The FIXER'S Guide to...

WEDGES

Written by **JOHN WOOD**

Designed by **AMY LI**

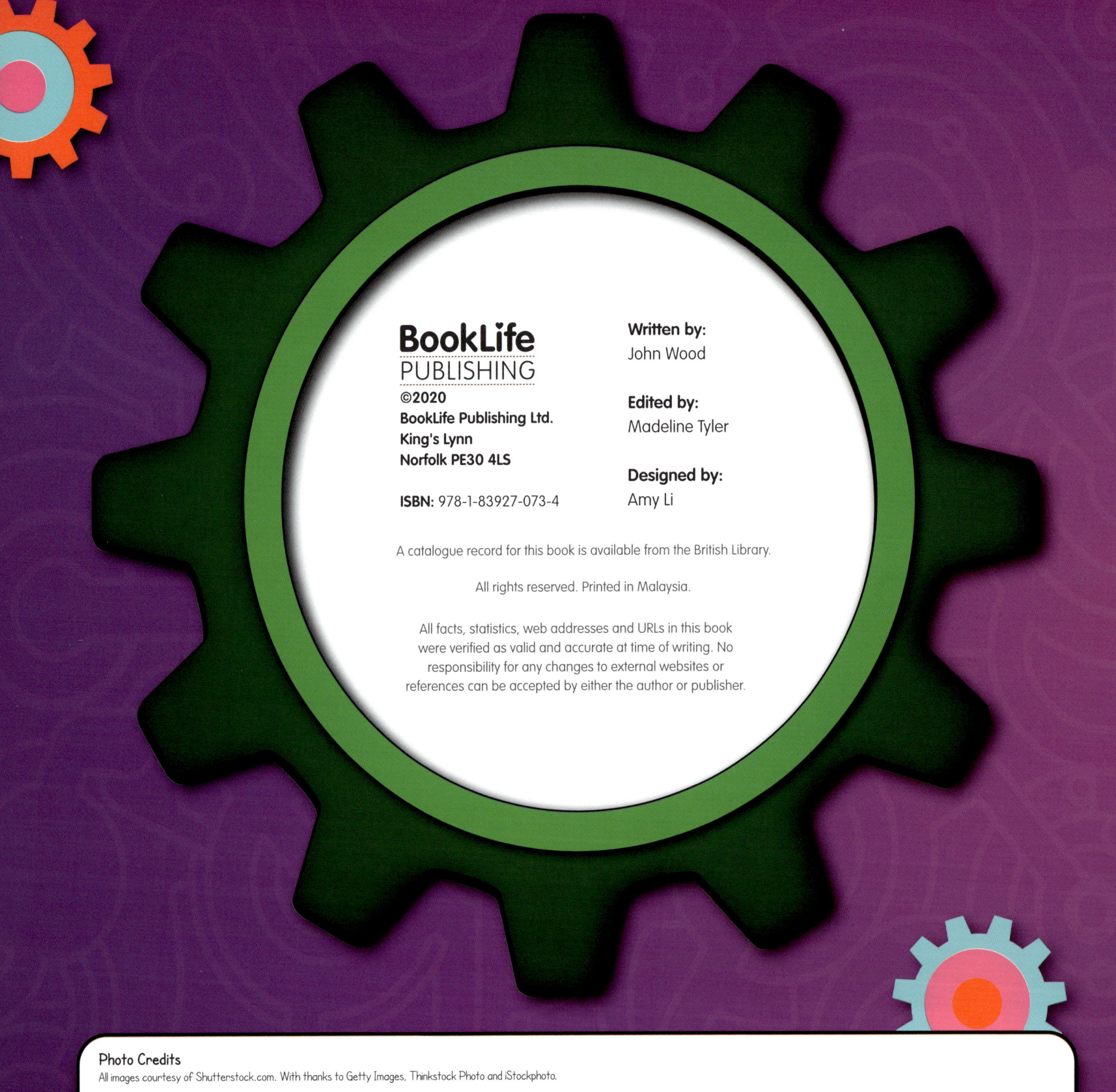

BookLife PUBLISHING

©2020
BookLife Publishing Ltd.
King's Lynn
Norfolk PE30 4LS

ISBN: 978-1-83927-073-4

Written by:
John Wood

Edited by:
Madeline Tyler

Designed by:
Amy Li

A catalogue record for this book is available from the British Library.

All rights reserved. Printed in Malaysia.

All facts, statistics, web addresses and URLs in this book were verified as valid and accurate at time of writing. No responsibility for any changes to external websites or references can be accepted by either the author or publisher.

Photo Credits
All images courtesy of Shutterstock.com. With thanks to Getty Images, Thinkstock Photo and iStockphoto.

Cover – Stock_VectorSale, Recurring images (cover and internals) – Guliveris (background pattern), Agor2012, robuart (cogs), Steve Paint (arrows). 4–5 – Aleutie, Quarta, Stock_VectorSale, Ico Maker, Pavel L Photo and Video. 6–7 – Daniela Pelazza, LeonidKos. 8–9 – Africa Studio, Bayurov Alexander, Celiafoto, Oleksandr Derevianko, Paradise On Earth, Toey Toey, tynyuk. 10–11 – Rinat Sultanov, brizmaker, sonia62. 12–13 – Hans Christiansson, Noerenberg. 14–15 – Pam Walker, Craig Russell. 16–17 – balipadma, jongcreative, Krasowit. 18–19 – grmarc (scissors), HardtIllustrations (glue). 22–23 – peart, Mascha Tace.

CONTENTS

PAGE 4   Meet the Fixer
PAGE 6   Wedges
PAGE 10   Parts of a Wedge
PAGE 12   How Does a Wedge Work?
PAGE 14   Singles and Doubles
PAGE 16   The Best Wedge
PAGE 18   Let's Build a Toy Crocodile
PAGE 24   Glossary and Index

Words that look like this can be found in the glossary on page 24.

MEET THE FIXER

Oh dear! What a mess — the Fixer is a very clumsy alien. Say sorry, Fixer.

Pfflblubwublee.

Believe it or not, the Fixer is the smartest being in the universe when it comes to machines.

A machine is an object that makes a job easier to do. The Fixer wants to teach you about one of the simplest types of machine: a wedge.

A stapler is a simple machine. So is a door.

WEDGES

A wedge is something that is very thick at one end and very thin at the other. Wedges can hold things together or split things apart.

Wedges are often in the shape of a triangle.

Wedges are often used to split something else apart. For example, an axe is a wedge. Axes are often used to split the wood apart.

The thin end of a wedge is often sharp.

Heuffflipughht.

Here are some more examples of wedges that people use.

Knife

Chisel

A doorstop is a wedge used to hold a door open.

A nail is a type of wedge.

Did you know that there is a type of wedge that you have, but the Fixer doesn't?

Flyblifflenyleugh.

That's right, Fixer. The answer is teeth.

Teeth split food apart.

PARTS OF A WEDGE

Many wedges are like two ramps stuck together. One end is thick and wide. The other is thin and sometimes sharp. It is the thin end that splits or holds something.

Thick end

Thin end

Something or someone must use force to move the wedge. For example, a person might use their strength to swing an axe into a tree.

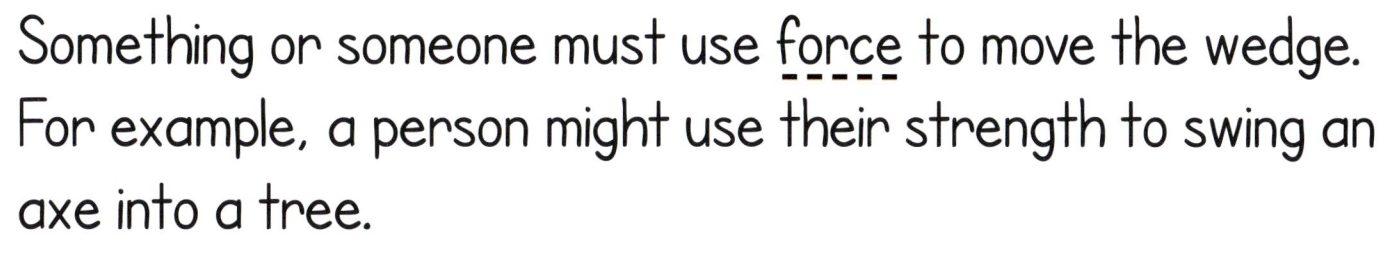

Sometimes wedges are moved by motors, such as this nail gun.

HOW DOES A WEDGE WORK?

A wedge changes the <u>direction</u> of the force. When a person swings an axe down, the bits of wood are moved sideways. Can you see how the direction of the force changes in the picture?

Sometimes the wedge is forced in by hitting it with another tool, such as a hammer.

It is much easier to swing an axe downwards than it is to pull wood apart. This is why a wedge is such a good simple machine. It makes the work much easier.

SINGLES OR DOUBLES

Wedges come in two types: single wedges and double wedges. In a double wedge, the force is redirected in two directions. Most of the wedges we have looked at so far have been double wedges.

In a double wedge, both sides go from thick to thin.

Doorstops and chisels are examples of single wedges. In a single wedge, one side goes from thick to thin, but the other side is flat. This means the force is only changed in one direction.

Thick

Thin

Flat side

HEUEBLUPHREE!

THE BEST WEDGE

Fixer, what makes a good wedge?

Fyrippleyripli.

Ah, interesting. The Fixer says it is to do with the distance between the thick end and the thin end, and how sharp it is.

The longer and sharper a wedge is, the less force it will take for the work to get done. A shorter wedge will need more force.

Good wedge!

LET'S BUILD A TOY CROCODILE

It is time to build! We will be using wedges to make a toy crocodile with teeth. Remember, teeth are a type of wedge.

YOU WILL NEED:

- 2 A4 sheets of green paper
- Glue
- Piece of cardboard
- 2 googly eyes
- Scissors
- Pen or pencil

You might need an adult to help you when using scissors and glue.

19

STEP 1

Fold one-third of one of the A4 sheets lengthways. Cover it in glue, and then fold the other side on top.

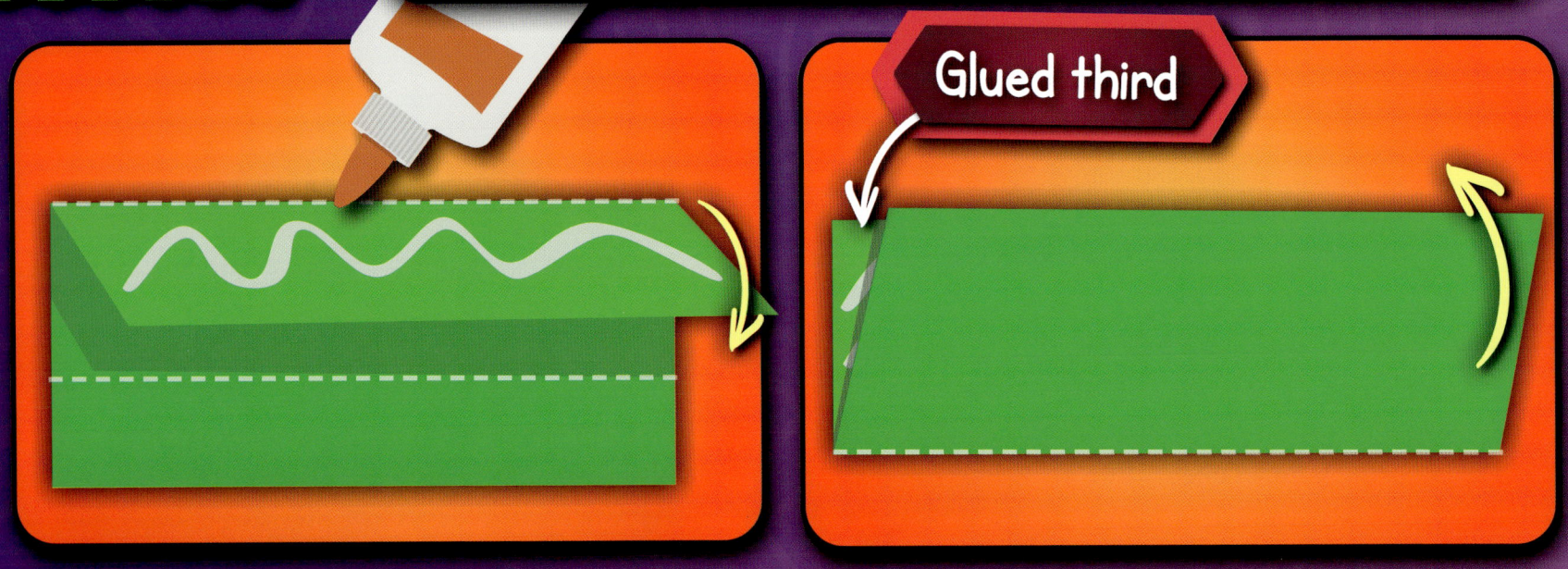

Glued third

STEP 2

Fold the paper so it is half as long. Take the loose ends and fold them back on themselves, so they touch the fold line.

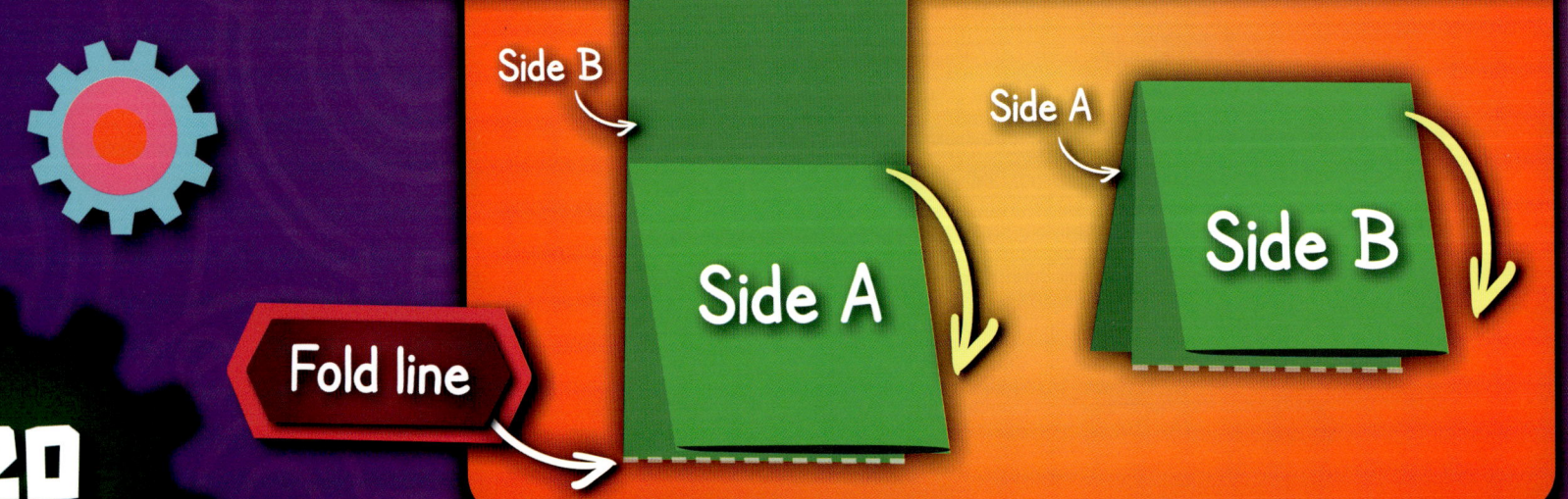

Side B

Side A

Fold line

Side A

Side B

STEP 3

Cut the other A4 sheet into thirds, lengthways. Take one strip and fold it back and forth until it looks like the picture.

STEP 4

Glue the two pieces together, like the picture. The holes of the first piece should be under the long strip.

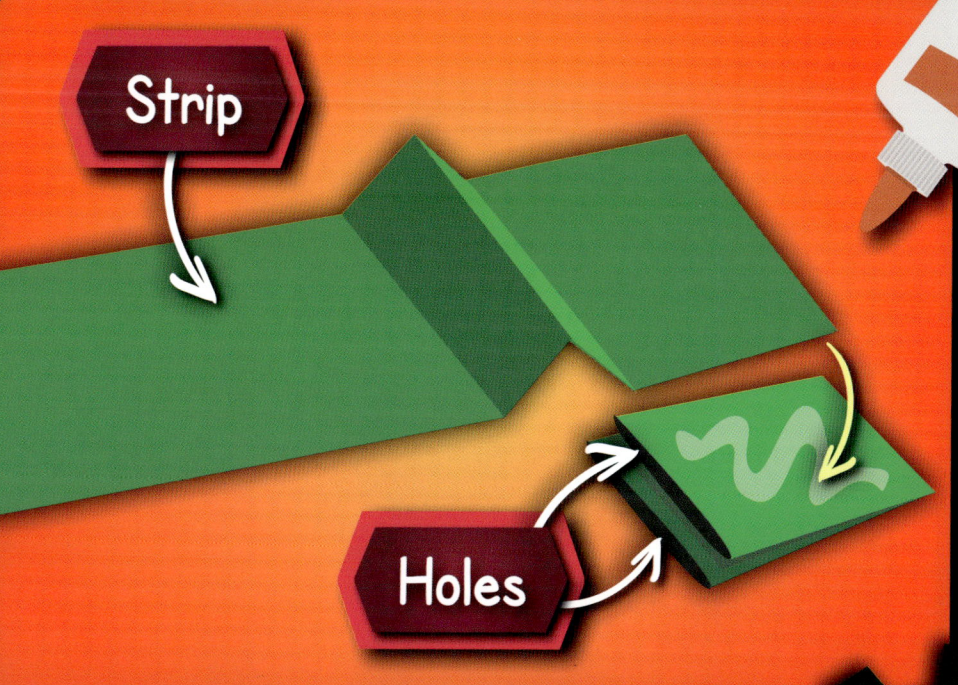

STEP 5

Glue two eyes onto the part that sticks up. Fold the long strip back and forth to make a zigzag and then cut it into a point to make the tail.

STEP 6

Cut two rows of spikes out of your cardboard. These are your teeth. Glue them to the front of the mouth, like the picture.

Fold back along the dotted line.

STEP 7

Put your fingers and thumb into the holes under the tail. Now you can make the crocodile bite.

STEP 8

Test out your crocodile on different materials. Can you bite into something soft?

GLOSSARY

direction	the place where something is moving
force	a push or pull on an object
motors	machines that move things
ramps	something that slopes up or down
redirected	changed direction
tool	an object used to do a certain job – it can usually be held in a person's hand
universe	the space that everything exists in, including planets, galaxies and stars

INDEX

axes 7, 11–13
force 11–15, 17
knives 8
people 11–12
splitting 6–7, 9–10
teeth 6, 10, 14–16
thick 6, 10, 14–16
thin 6–7, 10, 14–16
trees 11
wood 7, 12–13